W9-BKB-564

Alone at High Noon

A ZONDERVAN "REFLECTIONS" BOOK

at High Noon

Reflections on the Solitary Life

EMILE CAILLIET

ZONDERVAN PUBLISHING HOUSE
GRAND RAPIDS, MICHIGAN

ALONE AT HIGH NOON

Grand Rapids, Michigan

Library of Congress Catalog Card Number 74-133356

Grateful acknowledgment is expressed for permission to quote from *The Autobiography of Bertrand Russell* reprinted by permission of the Canadian publishers, McClelland and Stewart Limited, Toronto.

Printed in the United States of America

Gladys Burton has typed the manuscript of this little book with her usual care and unselfish devotion. May she find here the expression of my gratitude. E. C.

Contents

Foreword

A sense of solitariness continues to plague our world. For many of us and in many ways it threatens to become the most virulent disease of all ages. To be sure, the fact of being alone or of living alone like a recluse or hermit is in itself colorless. Only in the measure that it becomes a conscious longing for some impossible solution and turns into a dreary loneliness does it prove both harmful and painful. Indeed, he who is entirely alone by himself must watch for the point of seemingly no return where his aloneness begins to generate subjective feelings of isolation. Should he then merely be reacting to the flow of time and events? Obviously not. It should repay him a thousandfold to try and think through the implications of his solitude.

Alone at High Noon

1. ELECTIVE SOLITARINESS

1.

Elective Solitariness

An important reservation should be made at the outset of this inquiry, namely, that solitariness, the fact of being alone or of living alone, is neither good nor bad in itself as far as the wages of solitude are concerned.

Recluse and Hermit

The experiences of recluse and hermit illustrate this point. They show forth a solitariness practiced for its own sake as well as for an ideal deemed worthy of attainment.

Thus the man who has been acknowledged as the

thou wilt loathe it. If in the beginning of thy conversion thou art content to remain in it, and keep to it well, it will afterwards be to thee a dear friend, and a most pleasant comfort. (I, 20, 5)

A Secular Illustration

On the secular side, the classical illustration of a solitariness sought out for its own sake is that of Thoreau's *Walden*. Thoreau went to live alone in a hut at Walden Pond from July 4, 1845, to September 6, 1847. *Walden* was published in 1854. The reason Thoreau gives for going to the woods is that he wished to "live deliberately," to confront only the essential facts of life, and see if he could not learn what life had to teach, and not, when he came to die, discover that he had not lived.

In his section on "Solitude," he explains that he went and came with a strange liberty in nature, truly a part of herself. All the elements of nature proved unusually congenial to him. Every little pine needle seemed to expand and swell with sympathy and to befriend him. He did not feel lonesome. When asked whether he did not want to be nearer to other people, especially on rainy or snowy days and nights, he was tempted to reply: "This whole earth which we inhabit is but a point in space . . . Why should I feel lonely? Is not our planet in the Milky Way? . . .

What sort of space is that which separates a man from his fellows and makes him solitary? I have found that no exertion of the legs can bring two minds much nearer to one another."

At this juncture, his profession of faith in solitude came to full expression:

> What do we want most to dwell near to? Not to many men surely, the depot, the post-office, the bar-room, the meeting-house, the school-house, the grocery, Beacon Hill, or the Five Points, where men most congregate, but to the perennial source of our life, whence in all our experience we have found that to issue, as the willow stands near the water and sends out its roots in that direction. This will vary with different natures, but this is the place where a wise man will dig his cellar. . . .

In the personality of Thoreau we come into contact with a man who by faith and the skillful work of his hands had learned to live a life attuned to that of nature. In him we discover the presence of "that inward eye" which in the words of Wordsworth "is the bliss of solitude."

In Praise of Solitariness

Indeed there is such a reality as elective solitariness. The point, however, is that to enjoy its blessings one need not spend his life on top of a pillar, or seek refuge in a monastery or in a hut.

There is a solitariness which can be enjoyed among a few selected souls. Thus Thoreau himself tells us that he had three chairs in his house: one for solitude, a second one for friendship, and a third one for society. While society was accordingly most restricted, there remained a choice place for friendship, a highly selective type of friendship. I have read somewhere that only solitary men know the full joys of friendship. Others have their family; but to a solitary and an exile his friends are everything. Nay, solitude may be elected because it is a friend in itself. Thus Emerson, musing over the conduct of life, saw in solitude the safeguard of mediocrity. To him solitude was "to genius the stern friend." In the same vein James Lowell called solitude "the nurse of full-grown souls." To Milton a sweet retired solitude proved to be on occasion the best society, as short retirement urged sweet return.

Thus there are those choice souls who elect solitariness for the sake of its fruits. They do not find that any sacrifice is therein involved. It is in solitude that they are least alone. So say men like Byron and Gibbon in their own way. Wordsworth singles out a gracious, benign solitude as a source of relief "when from our better selves we have had too long." Shelley loved what he called "tranquil solitude," and such society as seemed to be made in the image of solitude. Even Charles Lamb in the part of a convalescent made merry with his solitariness: If there be a regal solitude, he exclaimed, it is a sick bed!

2. INTIMATIONS OF LONELINESS

2.

Intimations of Loneliness

With this chapter we come to forms of solitariness which make for unhappiness—and they are legion. How do they take shape, and what kind of feelings do they generate? But first, what overall mood may be said to characterize their expression? Can an early diagnosis of the sickness involved help direct our investigation?

The Case of Blaise Pascal

At the age of twenty-five Pascal had drawn the attention of scholars all over Europe. As a Christian, however, he felt that scientific labor was only praiseworthy to the extent that it was a quest for truth, but that it became sinful the very moment when, the means being taken for the end, the search for truth was turned into a search for oneself. In this he was following the teaching of Saint Augustine and of the Jansenists. As he saw it, it was impossible for God to be the end at all, if He were not also the principle. One of his fragments goes on with this terrible warning: "We lift our eyes on high, but lean upon the sand; and the earth will dissolve, and we shall fall whilst looking at the heavens." Might Pascal one day fall? It is so difficult to be in the world without being of the world!

Pascal could not limit himself, however, to the Scripture in his search for maxims of perfection: the passion for perfection laid hold of him no less intensely in the domain of science. The period of his life that was then opening up was to prove one of the most fruitful in scientific achievements. It was also to prove one of increased anguish. "Physical science," he wrote, "will not console me for the ignorance of morality in the day of affliction. But the science of ethics will always console me for the ignorance of the physical sciences." And Pascal entitled this fragment, *Vanity of the Sciences*.

There were other trials. His health was growing worse. For a time he was paralyzed from the waist down. He could not walk without the aid of crutches. His legs and feet were chilled, and they had to be kept wrapped in bandages soaked in brandy. The pains in his head and abdomen were more than he could bear. The physicians of the time made him take the most obnoxious medicaments. In his misery he kept saying over and over again that his infirmities were keeping him from his research, and this greatly distressed him. While his younger sister was enjoying the spiritual guidance and comfort of her Jansenist mentors, Blaise found only misunderstanding on their part. One of his accounts closes with an admission of helplessness on his part. A sense of inner solitude now overwhelmed him to the point that he would one day be called "this French Hamlet of Jansenism."

The death of his father dealt him a new blow. By then, however, Blaise had made new friends, worldly gentlemen in whose company he was now spending his time and who had become his models. In their company he undertook a journey to the Province of Poitou where he was initiated into the ways of the world. He even seems to have tried out dancing, for one of his fragments has it that to dance "we have to think carefully where we are going to put our feet"—which would seem to indicate that he never went far into his initiation.

The plain truth is that this experience of the world soon ended in a disillusioned and uneasy sense of solitude. He suddenly came to feel "a great contempt for the world" and "an almost unconquerable loathing for all persons in it." Having then set himself to consider the several kinds of restlessness that disturb men, and the perils and pains to which they expose themselves, which give rise to so many quarrels, passions, bold and often bad ventures, Pascal came to the conclusion that "all the unhappiness of men arises from one single fact, that they cannot stay quietly within four walls."

A Turning Point in Modern Solitude

No one, to my knowledge, has better illustrated modern solitude than Baudelaire. In his case, a unique sense of loneliness drives the soul to depths of Satanism. By then, Satan has become an immense symbol of cosmic evil, a sort of contemporary Ahriman whose activities become confused with those of the forces of nature. He is to be found in the fatality of things, in the brutal dynamic quality of matter, in the sobbing winds as in the raging tempest, in falling night as in coming death. Here then is modern solitude in its very essence—a bitterness at the bottom of our joys; the sensation that sometimes comes to one out of nothingness; again the deception of promises that lie, of happiness that ends in tears. The resulting experience of loneliness seizes man's whole being, and creates a frightful agony within him, stirring up the mud from the bottom of his whole being.

Baudelaire boasted of having invented the Satanic element in his poetry. Here again he did exaggerate, but this very exaggeration in itself is a form of Satanism. His opuscule *My Heart Laid Bare* reveals in man two simultaneous tendencies: one toward God—spirituality, which urges him toward the heights; and the other toward Satan—animality, which Baudelaire calls "a joy in descending." It is certainly this "joy in descending" that inspires in Baudelaire so many exaggerations of his dandyism, particularly that which I have just mentioned. Dante's muse saw Hell dreamily, writes d'Aurevilly; the muse of Baudelaire's *Flowers of Evil* drinks in it with quivering nostrils, like a horse that smells gunpowder. Dante's muse comes from Hell; Baudelaire's is going there. If the former is more venerable, the latter is perhaps more moving. Before Baudelaire's time the trouble had been in the mind; it now affected the heart with an aching sense of cosmic loneliness. Thus we arrive at a turning point in modern solitude. Here we must pause.

In Baudelaire we are concerned with a case of temperament which was probably influenced by the advanced age of his father at the time of his birth. The poet tells us in his *Posthumous Works* that even as a child he felt in his heart two contradictory sentiments: the horror of life and the ecstasy of life. "It is truly the case of a nervous laggard," he writes. Baudelaire further aggravated his condition by drug addiction. He was a member of the Haschichins Club, or hashish eaters, which met in the sumptuous atmosphere of Fernand Boissard's huge Louis XIV drawing room, frequented by Gautier and even Balzac. Baudelaire particularly enjoyed darvamesk, a fabulous dispenser of ecstatic hallucinations.

As if to make sure of his solitude, Baudelaire sought to emphasize his uniqueness. To astound people was the great preoccupation of the dandy in him. He handled paradoxes, hoaxes and lies with consummate art. He falsified his true face with pleasure and created an erroneous image of himself. He was the principal author of his own legend. It was he himself who wished to be considered a neurotic, a drug-addict, a semi-mad man. Leconte de Lisle's opinion of Baudelaire is well known: "He was a good chap who affected a ferocious grin, a writer born to be a classicist who churned his brain to discover the unusual." One always wonders how much to believe and how much to let go on this subject. This much is sure: he must have been terribly lonely to become the hero of the multiple stories which now amuse posterity.

For example, he told this would-be astounding tale: "I gave myself a thoroughly original concert last night. I tied a cat by its tail, head downward, before my window in such a way that its claws could scratch on the pane. I went to bed. I did not sleep, of course. Fortunately! No, you cannot imagine the singular and penetrating symphony furnished by the cat's mews and the sound of its claws on the window-pane. It was delicious!"

Whether Baudelaire's story is true or not does not matter. To think of such things one must be in a strange state of mind. It truly is a dandyism born of a sense of loneliness of soul. Did Baudelaire really split wood in his drawing room? Did he paint his hair green? Did he drag his mistress about by the hair at night? He boasted of it, and that suffices for us. Did he often sleep in the brown oak bed with neither footboard nor posts, shaped like a carved coffin? He owned it, and this fact alone is sufficiently eloquent. Baudelaire's dandyism betrays a tremendous void within.

Baudelaire painted himself in one of his short stories, *La Fanfarlo*, in the character of a poet who presents his book in homage to a beautiful and melancholy young woman. When she reproaches him for the disheartened character of his poetry: "Pity me," he replies, "or rather pity all of us, for I have many brothers of my kind. It is hatred of us all that has led us to these lies. It is through despair at not being able to be noble and beautiful by natural means that we have painted our faces so strangely." This young poet admits with pleasure that he possesses a depraved imagination. He loves deceits and artifice, and if God had confided nature's plan to him, he perhaps would have spoiled it all!

What contrary joy this is! To take the reverse of everything begins by being simple paradox, but this taste develops until it becomes unhealthy, unnatural. It is a sort of reversed activity that delights in being such. How can we account for a sense of solitude that can lead to such extremes?

La Fanfarlo was written in 1847. At this time

Baudelaire had already experienced pecuniary difficulties, and a moral exhaustion that in 1845 led him to beat his breast with a knife. The idea of suicide became an obsession with him; already the fear of madness haunted him. He was in this frame of mind when he published his *Flowers of Evil* in 1857. In a letter written January 23, 1862, one finds this confession: "I have cultivated my madness with joy and with terror. I now suffer from dizziness constantly, and today . . . I experienced a strange warning. I felt the wind of the wing of imbecility pass over me."

From the artificial we pass to the morbidly temperamental, into the realm of pathology. But Baudelaire's affliction had deeper roots; he suffered moral misery. He had been deeply perverted by the strange black Venus Jeanne Duval, whose acquaintance seems to have rendered him forever incapable of happiness, particularly with the delightful Mme. Sabatier. Certainly it was not the dandy who, in *My Heart Laid Bare*, made this true confession, which sounds like a page from Vinet: "After a debauch, one always feels more lonely, more deserted." The *Posthumous Works* are filled with such true confessions that we have the impression of touching Baudelaire's naked soul with our own: "The unique and supreme delight of love lies in the certainty of doing wrong."—"What is boring about love is that it is a crime in which one must have an accomplice." Who better than the lonesome Baudelaire has described the maliciousness of perverse love? "Do you hear these sighs, preludes to a tragedy of dishonor, these wails, these cries, these rattlings in the throat? Who has not proffered them, who has not irresistibly extorted them? Is there anything worse in the cross-examinations of torturers? These reversed sleepwalker's eyes, these limbs, whose muscles tremble and stiffen as beneath the action of a galvanic battery. Drunkenness, delirium and opium in their most violent reactions certainly do not furnish such frightful and curious examples. And the human face, which Ovid believed to be made to reflect the stars, there it is with no more than an expression of mad ferocity, or distended in a sort of death. Surely I should commit a sacrilege to apply the word 'ecstasy' to this kind of 'decomposition.' "

Solitude is a State of Soul

The preceding illustrations have shown that there is a great difference between being alone and being solitary. There is such a thing as solitude in the midst of a crowd—indeed this is one of the most virulent forms of solitude. On the other hand aloneness turns into a painful sense of solitude the moment it becomes conscious, aware of its own misery.

A divided soul soon turns into a lonely soul, as we have seen in Pascal's inner conflicts between dedication to science and a devotion to his Christian faith. Misunderstandings with other people added to his trial. Great indeed is the solitude of the man whose generous motivation is construed by others in terms of ulterior motives. Poor health, death in the family added to his ordeal.

It is most natural for a lonely soul to seek solace in worldly activities, to yield to the urge of being "elsewhere." It is a fact, however, that we shall find no one but ourselves along whatever path we take. We only know that which we are. If Socrates opens his door, he is sure to find Socrates asleep on the threshold, and to have an opportunity for being wise; but should Judas go out tonight, he is sure to meet . . . Judas, and to find an opportunity for betraying someone. It is noteworthy that Joan of Arc should hear the voices of angels, and Lady Macbeth the shrieks of witches. Should Pascal then go away on a trip to be initiated into the ways of the world, he too will meet . . . Pascal, and find new ways of being a lonely soul.

What then are we to make of Pascal's conclusion that "all the unhappiness of men arises from one single fact, that they cannot stay quietly within four walls"? Simply this—that when they at long last reach the refuge of these four walls, these men will find no one but themselves, complete with all the worries and lonely thoughts they used to entertain in the wide world! Our solitude is a part of us. It is a state of soul. We indulge in it wherever we are and wherever we go. To be sure, as aloneness implies absence of distraction, it is particularly conducive to introspection. Accordingly, to be hemmed in within four walls is likely to invite thoughts of solitude all the sooner—but this reservation implies merely a matter of timing. The basic fact remains, namely, that "to go places" is no way of curing our loneliness, for the simple reason that wherever we go we will find no one but ourselves waiting for us.

In the case of Baudelaire we come to grips with the dimension of the Demonic. John A. Mackay defines this tendency as "the pretension of anything that is purely finite to take the place of the infinite, together with the ruthless spirit and fateful consequences that accompany this pretension." It appears when an individual assumes the attributes of Deity, and in doing so becomes absolutely self-centered. Hence a proud self-assertion conducive to a transvaluation of all values, an enthrallment to evil, and a moral collapse, well-symbolized by these words of Milton's Satan: "Farewell remorse! All good to me is lost. Evil be thou my good." Indeed, what a Foreword to Baudelaire's *Flowers of Evil!*

According to Christian teaching, self-centeredness is the essence of sin. Thus the self-sufficiency of man is itself the full measure of his solitude. Such a man is no longer addressable or answerable. He becomes, as it were, infected by evil. There, at the core of his very being, he comes into contact with a deep layer of hidden, unborn forces; with the "collective unconscious" from which he emerges in a proud god-almightiness. Like *Faust's* Mephistopheles, he henceforth embodies the spirit which denies everything held precious in the world. His introverted thinking becomes increasingly oriented by the now infected subjective factor which in the last resort determines his judgment. Because external facts are no longer the origin and the aim of this type of thinking, as the introvert would often like to make it appear, there results a loss of contact with the objective reality of the things that are. Hence a tremendous sense of solitude in the subject even in the midst of the world of men and affairs.

Facts are now become of secondary importance for this kind of thinking. What apparently matters is the subjective idea, the inner vision of a primordial symbolical image. External happenings are meant to fit into, and fulfill, the framework involved in that image. An essential unconscious factor is thus shaped and formulated by the living symbol which ipso facto becomes the tool by which the imagination manipulates phantasies. Symbolic associations originating in the phantastic magic of childhood are accordingly reinforced and transmitted to the point of being perpetuated. In the case of Baudelaire, an aged father did not allow the child to become his parents' "little man." Possibly, the authoritative father figure proved too forbidding or even hostile to permit the child's solution of early conflicts. Hence the development of a sense of solitude may have laid the foundation for the abnormal forms of expressions we have witnessed in the adult. Indeed, solitude in infancy is a widespread phenomenon which casts its manifestations over the formative years of youth.

3. EARLY FORMS OF SOLITUDE

3.

Early Forms of Solitude

It is generally believed that childhood and youth are normally happy and carefree periods of life. There are only a few people who would regard them as solitary. And yet, keen observers have been led to dismiss such optimism as gratuitous. Thus Robert Louis Stevenson confesses that he was a great solitary when he was young, while the great psychologist William James goes as far as to say that solitude is actually the great source of terror to infancy.

Why should this be the case while babies and children in general are supposed to be the objects of so much affection and care on the part of the adult world? Who can be more secure than a little child?—

a remark currently put more as an exclamation than as a question. And yet, further investigation of the issue at hand provides an entirely different picture.

The Unwanted Child

There are many children who were unwanted even before they were born. Sigmund Freud submits among many others the case of a woman who had a dream meaning that she wished to see her only daughter (then seventeen years old) lying dead. With the help of the psychoanalyst, she discovered that while she was pregnant with that daughter she had actually cherished this death-wish. To quote from Freud's diagnosis of the case:

> The child was the offspring of an unhappy marriage, which ended in the speedy separation of husband and wife. Once when the child was as yet unborn the mother, in an excess of rage after a violent scene with her husband, beat her body with her clenched fists in order to kill the baby in the womb. How many mothers who today love their children tenderly, perhaps with excessive tenderness, yet conceived them unwillingly and wished that the life within them might not develop further; and have indeed turned this wish into various actions, fortunately of a harmless kind. The

later death-wish against beloved persons, which appears so puzzling, thus dates from the early days of the relationship to them.

(*A General Introduction to Psycho-analysis,* Thirteenth Lecture)

Freud further cites the case of a father who similarly had wished the death of his eldest and favorite child. His marriage had proved a disappointment. When the child was still an infant, he had often thought that if the little creature who meant nothing to him were to die, he would again be free and would make better use of his freedom.

Let us now look at the side of the infants concerned who somehow become aware of their being unwanted—surely the most painful solitude. There are in families many illustrations of similar impulses of hate which have not been purged by a growing affection, but actually continue to play their part. The impression left on the children concerned is all the more vivid and painful as they love themselves first of all. Only later on may their ego allow them to experience some kind of love of others, that is, of willing sacrifice. Even then, such love may prove to be on their part the price they have to pay for being loved. In the last analysis, self-love remains the rule.

And we have already seen that self-love is the great breeder of solitude.

Not only does the child learn how to love through his own egoism, but there are many instances when he does not love at all. Thus infants of two and a half to four years old, see a rival when the new baby arrives. Even a death wish appears in the remark that little brother or sister may again be taken away the way he or she came. No wonder such dramas will put in a reappearance in later dreams or life situations. Bernard Shaw is said to have remarked that "If there is anyone whom a young English lady hates more than her mother it is her elder sister."

Lonely Infants in a World of Giants

We adults appear to the child under age three as giants twenty-five feet tall, and he is at our mercy. Thus he lives in a world strange to us. We may punish him for "lying" about what happens in this world, but such a misinterpretation on our part can only add to his sense of loneliness.

The language we omnipotent giants speak, the demands it expresses, do not make sense to the infant. They are immediately construed as the exigencies of all-powerful people who can either gratify the child's every wish, or simply annihilate him. An adult is accordingly all good or totally bad. At the moment, the good person cannot do anything bad, neither can the bad person do anything good. While the real father and mother are so apprehended, the same is true of other people. Thus the child under three has, in addition to his good or bad father and mother, phantastic fathers and mothers. There is nothing final in this classification to be sure. It mostly depends on what those concerned are doing at the present time, and the infant treats them accordingly. Either he loves them above anything else or he hates them intensely. He is an extremist. No wonder he is misunderstood. His solitude is difficult for us to evaluate.

Jean Piaget, who may be called the father of our new understanding of the infant child, has been influenced in his research on the primitive mind by the monumental work of Lucien Lévy-Bruhl. Many points of contact between the two types of mentality—that of the primitive and that of the child—have thus been discovered. Nay, in his study of the child's conception of causality, of the world, of his language and thought, of play, dreams and imitation, Piaget has brought to light between the mind of the child and that of the adult, a basic dichotomy which in many ways echoes that uncovered by Lévy-Bruhl between the mind of the primitive and that of the white Mediterranean adult. In both cases, as a result, we witness the making of profound misunderstandings which isolate children as well as natives from common ways of feeling and apprehending the world in which we live. Needless to insist that in both cases we accordingly see at work the making of an inner solitude.

Problem Teenagers

Contrary to some current sociological thinking, a large proportion of problem teenagers come from overprivileged homes. These blase youngsters who have everything their own way are born to be lonely. They are often apt to add up to a dead weight once they allow themselves to indulge in any kind of membership. Being well cared for in their wealthy suburban home they seemingly have no problem. Neither do they care for any kind of commitment.

And yet, contrary to expectation, the public at large does not realize the unbelievable degree of emotional tension to which many such teenagers are subject. Thus I have come across the case of a high school junior who came from a commuter town in

Connecticut and was so emotionally tense that he suffered from a bleeding ulcer. He had to undergo an operation. Eight feet of his intestine were removed. It turned out that he was plagued by psychosomatic problems at least partially due to family blow-ups and academic difficulties; he was also troubled by problems in youthful romance.

The aggravating feature in such instances proceeds from adult attitudes. Success-mad parents and other community leaders are apt to distort and actually discourage personal commitment, however praiseworthy the cause. This they do in fact before and after commitment is made: "Don't let this thing ruin your chances of making yourself a success!" Here I think of a certain high school coach who discouraged boys from joining a Christian organization because its activities would interfere with their athletic career. Most of these fellows stopped attending, with the result that membership in the association that had counted over a hundred was cut down to some thirty.

General apathy on the part of adults is mostly at fault in all this. There is apathy about personal commitment, about discipline; there is tremendous apathy when it comes to financial sacrifice to see a child to camp, a family pay their rent, or to feed an orphan somewhere in the wide world. Thus an insidious vacuum is created which only boredom can fill. Rejection of and indifference to any general initiative arc its firstfruits.

The solitary teenager is naturally tempted to seek gratification in sex relations. The question as to what is right and what is wrong is one of the first he is likely to ask. Most of the time his inquiry is perfectly candid. He just does not know the answer. He is groping for one. His natural urges crave satisfaction—to what extent should they be satisfied? The paraphernalia of civilization—movies, radio, TV, books, magazines, newspapers, advertisement—expose the readiness of a good many adults to do as they please in the matter. Traditional standards seem to be denied by the evidence our culture supplies. What right do adults have, then, says a youngster to himself, to force arbitrary limitations on the younger generation? This much is sure: mere moralistic pronouncements will be seen as arbitrary encroachment and accordingly ignored. Ignored, that is, unless the older person, man or woman, forces respect by the quality of his own character—and unless his motivation is apprehended as born of undeniable friendly interest.

A genuinely friendly approach on the part of

someone a teenager has learned to love and admire marks the first step toward a solution. And this is all the more true when the teenager, boy or girl, *has* to marry. It is a well-known fact that the proportion of pregnancies in our high school population has reached frightening figures.

It is commonplace evidence that teenagers think of marriage in the measure as they are lonesome. They crave the love and attention they may not find at home. The frequency of such marriages in many ways bespeaks the measure of the youngster's solitude. There is clear evidence from counseling that the prospect of finding a husband proves infinitely more attractive to young women than that of illicit sex relations. Furtive intercourse, under a sense of guilt and fear, often turns out to have been disappointing to a girl. The admission is frequent: "I got nothing out of it"—though this may occasionally hide an effort to minimize the gravity of the transgression. Boys, as a rule more positive in their evaluation, are sometimes found to be thus for the sake of boasting of their masculine powers, in spite of hidden frustration. In general, adolescent experimentation in sexual matters gives rise to self-analysis and self-criticism amounting to disappointment or even disgust.

Lonesomeness of the Asphalt Jungle

Nothing can spell solitariness more than great city jungles such as the lower East Side of New York. There the atmosphere is one of stale smells, soulless sounds, and faded hopes. Streets and dark alleys take their toll; gang pressure does its damage. Fellows who had begun to see the light are soon sucked back by the prevailing forces of evil. Alcohol and narcotics knock off even the most promising.

As we move on to the asphalt jungle and transpose the current pranks of teenagers to the current practices of real "tough guys," what we get is no longer episodic brushes with a law-abiding citizenry, but a new code of morality. Four teenagers recently admitted stealing three late-model automobiles. They stripped the cars, sold the parts, and used the proceeds to "soup up" their own hot rods. One teenager mentioned by the Manager of the National Auto Theft Bureau thus boasted that he could remove a car's transmission (worth about $260) in eight minutes. About a thousand cars are stolen every day in the United States, and judging from previous experience, the FBI estimates that teenagers may be responsible for approximately sixty-five per cent of that figure.

The overall why of this sordid situation is summed up in the ultimate solitude of the youngsters concerned, and the same admittedly takes varied forms of expression. For instance, it is fair to admit that teenagers have financial problems. Unemployment among those who quit school is high. Yet motivation strikes deeper, says Ray M. King—and he ought to know, since the National Auto Theft Bureau of which he is the manager is supported by about 350 insurance companies. "A lot of teenagers steal cars because they think it is the smart thing to do; it shows their pals they are not 'chicken'," he points out. That is, they steal cars for the sake of getting out of themselves; for the same sort of reason as gives them a spurious sense of power from the motor's roar, or makes them feel their girls are impressed when the noise climaxes in "gunning." Indeed solitude *has* many faces!

The city jungle type of teenager is actually found in a crowd—in a famous gang of he-men if he turns out to be someone. Since he has nowhere else to go, his hangout is the sidewalk. He may occasionally smile, but his is not a smile of hope; there is nothing for him to hope for. Under a crushing weight of boredom or a craving for popularity at any cost, he will attempt the craziest feats, such as breaking open a hydrant and shooting beer cans on the stream of water. When his pent-up feelings are too much to be relieved by horseplay, or the thought of an empty future proves unbearable, or grim pressure from the gangs proves irresistible, a shot of heroin becomes the temptation—and soon the addiction.

There is actually at work in the contemporary teenager an urge to experiment with intoxication. I do not refer here to alcohol, although FBI statistics are terribly eloquent as to the number of those who are arrested for drunkenness, driving while intoxicated, and generally violating liquor laws—figures higher than those referring to the number of arrests of teenagers for robbery, all types of assault, prostitution, other sex offenses, gambling, and narcotics violations. My point is the increasing use of any kind of substance that works as a narcotic.

The latest fad in this regard has been glue-sniffing, an addiction that damages vital organs and may even cause death. The youngsters squeeze model glue into cloths, and inhale. The fumes from quick-drying solvents in the glue, such as toluene and acetone, produce an intoxicating effect which is likely to lead to violence. There is, for example, the well-authenticated case of a fourteen-year-old boy who sniffed five tubes of glue in a day. He attacked a woman and forced her out of her car, then drove off and smashed into three others. To pass "anti-sniffing" laws as some towns have done does not reach to the roots of the situation.

The new teenage structures which are now coming into their own in semi-depleted areas, and in the concrete jungle of many of our major cities, do call for creativity and freshness of approach. The ultimate enemy is the lonesomeness of teenagers whose parents too often have no time for them.

The Hippie World

Were we to judge in terms of shaggy long-haired appearance, of the bearded look of youthful nomads, of their use of marijuana and LSD, a presentation of the Hippies of our day would prove a fitting appendix to the preceding section. Once more we would have found boredom and distress at work in the making of solitude. Yet oversimplification should then have dogged our steps.

The more one observes the Hippie world of our time, the more does it appear as a protest against a tense environment made all the more tragic by police raids; against a dreary kind of life which has lost the sense of simple pleasures; actually against cultural forms which drag along the moorings of the past. Let not the handout-seeking, wandering element involved in the Hippie movement lead one to condemn the whole of it as made up of a bunch of anarchistic beatniks wont to get "high" on mescaline.

To be sure, loneliness has played its part in the rise of the movement, but there has also been at work a purposeful desire to develop a community spirit freed from false needs and values, and cultivating genuine people-to-people sort of contacts. Thus new Hippie communities have been established in remote areas throughout the West where women make their own bread and their own clothes, where a genuine return to nature restores the value of primal pleasures amid a minimum of laws and regulations. Even where drugs are used, their consumption would at times seem to be motivated by an urge to rip from one's mind the falseness of obsolete cultural forms. In other words, there looms up a creative element in the older, most stable Hippie communities, and this promising aspect should not be undervalued by fair observers.

4. LONESOMENESS AT NOON

4.

Lonesomeness at Noon

Let us all admit that we have our moments of lonesomeness, and this for reasons that may well escape us at the moment. Rupert Brooke thus writes of a voyage he made a number of years ago. As he was leaving Liverpool, he felt lonely. Everyone seemed to have people to see them off. So he went back on shore and found a dirty little boy, who was unoccupied and said his name was William.

"Will you wave me if I give you sixpence, William?" asked Brooke. "Why, yes," replied William. This was obviously an easy way to earn some money. Rupert Brooke gave the boy sixpence and then went back on board the vessel. As Brooke watched, William leaned over the railing of the landing stage and waved. Now and then he shouted indistinct messages in a shrill voice. And as the vessel slid away, the last object that Brooke saw was a small boy faithfully waving a handkerchief. Brooke added these words: "So I got my sixpence worth and my farewell—dear William."

Dehumanization of Man

There is such a thing as a solitude inherent in professional involvement. I think here of the man who for days, weeks, months, and years, automatically performs the same kind of duty on the assembly line. What of his sense of solitude?

Some years ago—but it might have been yesterday—a leading newspaper in one of our big cities carried the report of a suicide. The man was up in years; he was a widower; all his family were gone; and he lived alone. He left a note stating that he had worked for nearly fifty years on the assembly line in a large factory, and during all that time no one had said whether his work was good, bad or indifferent. He was unable to stand his loneliness any longer. Truly, the man on the assembly line has been slowly transformed into a machine, progressively dehumanized.

Come the day when the monotony of it all becomes too much, and he indeed may take his life. Who can put into words the deadly monotony of work on the assembly line with men standing on the borderline between the human and the mechanical? The same set-up, the same motions of the body, the same outcome of production! Indeed, what amount of solitude is involved in such a drudgery!

It may be argued that the example quoted in the above paragraph involved an older man who had lost his wife, and whose children had left the home, and that *these* factors were responsible for the suicide. Such factors will indeed be taken up in this present chapter, but in the case under consideration their cumulative effect may be said to have been merely added to the distress of the assembly line.

According to the latest figures, provided by the World Health Organization, and available at the time of this writing, suicides in the United States alone represented 16.3 per 100,000 for men, and 6.1 for women—a total of 15,490 on the one hand, and 6,017 on the other. Now, the general consensus is that the most prevalent cause of suicide is a sense of loneliness in those who take their life, and this, admittedly was the case for the man on the assembly line we have given as an illustration. The other factors in his decision had merely helped bring his crisis to a head.

The same remark may be made for the derelicts who make toys, with only a bowl of cafeteria cereal to look forward to on Christmas Eve. The city may well laugh but suicides are on the rise. Some of these men actually are afraid to go home for Christmas. One of them is quoted as having said to the manager of the toy projects for Bowery derelicts: "I don't think I am strong enough to call my children. I have been accustomed to loneliness for so long that if I got together with my kids and had a warm time, I don't think I could take it."

Again I think of the salesman who is continually away from home. I have spoken to a number of such men who have told me of the dreariness of motel rooms in the evening, and especially at weekends. All they seem to look forward to is the day of retirement when it will all be over. But then, what will the overall prospect look like?

Should such men go on strike they have to face a misery in reverse. Said one of the strikers against General Electric who was interviewed recently: "What gets me is that as I stay at home all day long I don't know what to do with myself." In one form or another, then, lack of purpose would seem to be at the root of solitude.

Solitude Inherent in All Forms of Alienation

We may well pause to think, as we are confronted by the latest United States statistics on marriages and divorces, namely, 2,059,000 marriages and 582,000 divorces—a rate of 10.3 per 1,000 population for the calendar year 1968.

Indeed we live in days of many broken marriages. No longer do those concerned think of matrimony as a vocation, a partnership both of life and for life, meant to be a lifelong union. They have forgotten the glorious day of their wedding to which they had so keenly looked forward; or rather they now look back to that day with misgivings, as if it had not been meant to be the beginning of something better than itself, better even than courtship, and different from it. Life then had been partaken of to the uttermost. The clear-sightedness of mutual affection had accordingly become the true reality for both partners. Together they had over the years shared with children and friends a kindness which actually strengthened and deepened their love for one another. What a sense of growing loneliness had come over them, as these realities of all reality had faded away! Think of the tremendous vacuum in their lives!

The main point of the drama only comes out as we realize that the fact of divorce constitutes merely a climax; that actually months, years, nay, decades of misery may have intervened before that climax was reached. We may therefore ponder over the long periods of mutual solitude involved in so-called "grounds for divorce," namely, adultery, cruelty, desertion, non-support, alcoholism, felony, impotency, pregnancy at marriage, drug addiction, fraudulent contract, and yet other causes. Besides, what are we to think of the inevitable repercussions of a troubled marriage among the children? How many long days and nights of anguish for them, as they instinctively feel the chill that has come over their home life!

In all such instances there is on the part of those concerned a great deal of brooding, of whiling away time in the measure as it has lost significance—of actually "killing" time to hide the fact of loss of purpose. The common saying of the situation, the one which is used as a would-be explanation, if not a means of strategy at the hour of adultery is likely to be: "I am misunderstood at home"—another way of saying "I am lonely." Such *ennui* is fatal. It may on occasion trigger the substitutes of club membership, cocktail parties, or clandestine activities. Its aftermath nevertheless is an unbearable solitude.

Loneliness Involved in the March of Time

The inflexible march of time causes us to go through dramatic experiences of solitude. There is, for example, the day when we see a son or a daughter off to college. We then keenly feel the wrench of the departure. We know that henceforth the child will make its own way through life, run the risks of disappointments and accidents without our being around to provide protection and help.

Again there comes the day when we give away a daughter in marriage. We actually do not *know* this young man. All we seem to know is that he is becoming a substitute for us. Will he ever understand the girl the way we do? How hopeful yet distressed we feel as we walk down the steps of the chapel where our great sacrifice has come to consummation! And what a sense of solitude in our heart as we drive home alone! Now the two will go through trials and satisfactions on their own. Indeed they must live apart from us; if only they could live close enough so that they can be seen often, our loneliness should be more bearable.

Another kind of exercise in solitude becomes our lot when we learn of the passing of an old friend or comrade—an experience which becomes only too frequent as we grow older. Nay, our own generation, we realize, is beginning to fade away. Then we may well make our own the confession of Thomas Moore:

> When I remember all
>   The friends so linked together
> I've seen around me fall
>   Like leaves in wintry weather,
> I feel like one
> Who treads alone
> Some banquet hall deserted,
>   Whose lights are fled,
>   Whose garlands dead,
> And all but he departed!
> Thus in the chilly night
>   Ere slumber's chain has bound me,
> Sad Memory brings the light
>   Of other days around me.

At such moments the coming solitude of old age looms up as a warning in the deserted home.

The Crisis of Retirement

In the consideration of loneliness involved in the march of time, a special section should be reserved for the crisis of retirement. All that has been said in the previous paragraphs about the dehumanization of man in our industrial and economic set-up does not alter the fact that retirement does constitute a crisis in a man's life.

The worker who overnight finds himself unoccupied is likely to become apologetic for being found around the house. If unattended in his idleness, it may soon cause him to lose his self-respect and sense of worth. He may find himself ignored. Should he have occupied a position of leadership, those who found themselves "under him" have now begun to form new relationships with another "boss." His own name is less and less often mentioned in conversations. He is no longer recognized as an authority. He has lost prestige, if not face. He finds himself more and more alone, both at home and abroad.

Unless he makes up his mind to form new relationships, he discovers that he has henceforth no place to go. Avoiding previous companions and seemingly being avoided by them, he no longer frequents the old meeting-places. In a way he would be embarrassed to be seen there. How would he then justify his presence? Or if he did happen to go to the old "joint," he would be likely to be met by expressions of surprise. Even should these be well meant, he might interpret them otherwise.

In the long run, it might seem to him that after all he did enjoy the part he played in producing something useful or creating something beautiful. Did he not boast about such things? Nay, did he not take pride in his connection with the firm or institution that employed him? Colleges and universities acknowledge this situation by granting a man the title *Emeritus*. Industrial or commercial organizations do not. And so the retiree has to blow his own trumpet.

What is he good for now, anyway? To take care of a fixture in the kitchen, to go shopping, to do errands, to answer an occasional letter—but even the postman seems to have stopped passing by. Again, unless he does something about his new situation he is no longer of service to others, as was the case while he was employed.

And so the hours become ever longer, especially during the afternoon when TV programs are not at their best. Our man is increasingly bored. And being bored is a terrible experience. It is then that we realize that seats can be hard. We wonder at the number of muscles, nay, of bones that exist in our body. An intellectual begins to realize what Bergson meant when he said that time, as measured by the mechanism of our instruments, corresponds to no reality whatsoever; that if there be any reality involved in the notion of time it must be that of duration, an inner experience which makes us feel that there *are* short hours and long hours—and the hour during which we are being bored, lonely to the extreme, is indeed a long one. Did not work, after all, help make time pass?

It certainly did, but now our man has lost the sense of purpose which somehow undergirded the busyness of those years of activity. He is alone.

5. THE ADVANCING SHADOW

5.

The Advancing Shadow

Animals die; man *has* to die, and it makes all the difference. This fact looks ever larger and more impressive as we grow older. Within the uncanny perspective of old age we find ourselves increasingly confronted by the advancing shadow which bespeaks utter solitude. For we die alone.

The Solitude of Old Age

Our own death is the one personal fact which we can predict with absolute certainty, and it admittedly is a supremely tragic fact, a universal fact inherent in the very structure of Nature.

We have often labored under a sense of bewilderment, or irreparable loss, and of resulting loneliness as we silently stood before the remains of a friend. How could a thing like this be possible? We actually resented the evidence, yet the evidence was there, staring us in the face.

What then shall we say of the death of a life partner? Then the one who has been left behind partakes in the heart-rending experience evoked by William Dean Howells:

> The first night, when at night I went about
> Locking the doors and windows everywhere,
> After she died, I seemed to lock her out
> In the starred silence and the homeless air.

What about our own death, then? What does it mean to us? In the Ingersoll Lecture he gave at Harvard University on April 14, 1942, Douglas V. Steere asked this question in his own name, realizing that what he had come to identify as his permanent possessions would be stripped from him insofar as the medium of his body was concerned:

> My family will be taken away, my vocational position will in a few short weeks or months be given to another, my dreams and plans for the things I would accomplish for my fellows must now be relinquished

> to others, my possessions must go: my house will be sold or rented or passed into the hands of others, any income that I may have will go to others, my books will distribute themselves into the libraries of others . . . I must give up what Francis of Assisi called Brother Ass. I must be stripped of my body. This may be a painful operation not only in the physical pangs of death but because all of these other possessions of mine clutch the body tightly as their one hope of preservation.

The clear outcome of such cogitations comes to a head in a sense of quiet desperation, in what-is-the-good-of-it-all attitude—nay, in the exclamation of the book of Ecclesiastes: "Vanity of vanities, says the Preacher, vanity of vanities; all is vanity." What is the use of new undertakings? Even the daily routine of life loses significance, and the very suggestion of adopting a hobby sounds like a joke.

Dr. Glenn Beyer, director of the Cornell University Housing Research Center, recently studied the living habits of older Americans. He and his colleagues were surprised at the state of abandonment of the facilities provided for old folks. Only one percent of the elderly interviewed made any use of such activities as woodworking, photography, coin, stamp, and other collections. To quote from the President's Council on Aging, 1964, published by the United States Government Printing Office under the title, *On Growing Older*, (p. 123):

> Without valid mental and physical activity to fill their time, the opportunity is open for older people to dwell upon themselves at an age when it is least likely to help. A life empty of things to do, mental or physical, leaves a vacuum in which there is room for worry about normal declines of age, and it may have serious mental implications. Psychiatrists and psychologists find that older people frequently become hypochondriacs.

Among highly cultured people, the personal decision that they are through with everything takes on the shape of cosmic despair. Thus in his recently completed biography, Bertrand Russell, then on the borderline of the hundred-year-old mark, looked ahead to the specter of human misery and ultimate obliteration:

> We stand on the shore of an ocean, crying to the night and the emptiness; sometimes a voice answers out of the darkness. But it is the voice of one drowning; and in a moment the silence returns. The world seems to me quite dreadful; the unhappiness of many people is very great, and I often wonder how they all endure it. To know people well is to know their tragedy: it is usually the central thing about which their lives are built. And I suppose if they did not live most

of the time in the things of the moment, they would not be able to go on. (Quoted from *Christianity Today*, November 21, 1969)

Truly an outcry of cosmic solitude!

Cosmic Solitude

There sooner or later looms up an abyss of uneasiness at the core of human destiny. Earnest souls know what Francis Bacon meant when he said that men indeed fear death as children fear to go into the dark. Whether a man lifts up his gaze to survey the surrounding landscape or becomes aware of a pattern belonging in the warp and woof of the roaring loom of history, his curiosity soon turns into mingled surprise and anxiety; nay, into unmitigated anguish.

Time is growing short. Death may be near. The wind of eternity strikes his face. What is the possible meaning of all this *for him* at a higher level of existence? Is there a meaning to it all? Is there anywhere any ultimate sure foundation? Any sense to this striving which does not seem to achieve anything beyond the bodily existence of Francis of Assisi's Brother Ass? For the time being, alas, there seems to be only weary conjecture groping for some kind of stable certainty.

Thus, man's disheartening sense of cosmic solitude has been expressed by Pascal in striking ways: "The eternal silence of those infinite spaces frightens me," he exclaimed. And again:

> "What is man in Nature? A cypher compared with the Infinite, an All compared to Nothing, a Mean between zero and all. Infinitely unable to grasp the extremes, the end of things and their principle are for him hopelessly hidden in an impenetrable secret, for he is equally unable to see the Nothing whence he springs, and the Infinite in which he is swallowed up."

And again:

> "We sail over a vast expanse, ever uncertain, ever adrift, carried to and fro. Whatever point we think to fix and fasten ourselves to shifts and leaves us; and if we pursue it, it escapes our grasp, slips away, fleeing in eternal flight. Nothing stays for us. That is our condition, natural, yet contrary to our inclination; we have a burning desire to find a sure resting place and a final fixed basis whereon to build a tower rising to the Infinite; but our whole foundation cracks, and the earth yawns to the abyss."

However dimmed and blurred the vision within, there is on the part of mortal man an awareness of true greatness. Going straight to the core of such a stubborn, or should I say, noble defiance, we find its motivation in part in the fact that, somehow, a man cannot endure to be despised. Whatever one may say of him, whatever he may say to himself as to the radical uncertainty of his ways, there is something within him which calls him onward and upward. At the very moment when confinement is visited upon him, a lump will choke his throat and cause him to set his face against the baleful decree.

A man wants freedom from the possible self-delusion invited by a sense of cosmic solitude. He refuses to distinguish between what is practicable and what is true. He demands an answer—and he is in dead earnest about it. What is more, he is ready to rise to the occasion. And all the rest is literature to the weary mortal who has read all the books, only to be confronted around the corner by that ugly fact of Nature which Nature hides so well—namely, death.

Gethsemane

Surely the drama of cosmic solitude reached its climax in the garden of Gethsemane where "a Man of sorrows, and acquainted with grief" faced death in awful loneliness. He saw the great Passion ahead and looked into its very heart. The prospect was most frightening. Yet an astonishing strength of purpose dominated His whole being. Faced by an awful alternative, He chose to do the will of God which implied the emptying of the cup that confronted Him in all its bitterness.

Truly it was not a human hand that presented Him with a prospect of torture, but an almighty hand, and He Himself should be almighty to endure it. His three closest friends were there with Him, but they were asleep, and it was in vain that He sought at least a small measure of comfort from them. And so He was left alone without the slightest pity or understanding on the part of man. Indeed, what a solitude was His at that moment, a loneliness full of grief in the horror of the night! It is noteworthy that at this point the historical record for the first time registers a complaint on the part of Jesus, as if His pain had become too great for Him to bear: "My soul is sorrowful, even unto death." For the first time also we see Him seeking the companionship and comfort of men, but this is denied Him. His disciples continue to sleep.

To us, the most surprising thing about Jesus' reaction to their seeming indifference is that, far from viewing His own condition in terms of universal abandonment, He considers only the spiritual peril to which His three friends expose—not Himself, but themselves. His warning to them is for the sake of their own safety. There is only on His part warm tenderness and concern on their behalf, and this, in the face of their ingratitude.

He asks that the bitter cup may pass away from Him, but He does so with utter submission to the will of God. Again He asks that the ordeal come if need be for the salvation of men, and He does so with utter dedication. Thus He willfully enters into agony. And what an agony! His biographers employ most unusual words to express adequately the innermost nature of it. In so doing they convey the impression that language has to be taxed to the extreme to convey an adequate expression: He was sore amazed. He was very heavy. His soul was exceeding sorrowful, even to the point of death. He prayed with strong crying and tears in utter loneliness. The impression left us is that there is something eternally unique about such an ordeal of sore amazement, great heaviness of spirit, and bloody sweat. In the darkness beyond it we reach the apex of solitude.

In the words of Pascal, "Jesus will be in agony even unto the end of the world; we must not sleep during all that time."

6. A TRANSFIGURED SOLITARINESS

6.

A Transfigured Solitariness

When in the same night Jesus of Nazareth hangs from the cross and Judas Iscariot hangs from a tree, death is not the same for both. The issue of cosmic purpose is the crucial issue we must face to reach any worthwhile conclusion regarding the meaning of solitude.

Life Has Only Two Roads

We have been dealing thus far with what people call "the natural course of life." Matthew Arnold has summed up that "natural course of life" in the well-known verse of *Rugby Chapel:*

Most men eddy about
Here and there—eat and drink,
Chatter and love and hate,
Gather and squander, are raised
Aloft, and hurl'd in the dust,
Striving blindly, achieving
Nothing; and then they die.

That "natural course" implies a great deal of delusion, however; and the greatest delusion of all is to believe that there are many varieties of life and purpose. The number of them seems to decrease, like Balzac's famous magic skin, as time passes. The plain truth, the immense and all-important truth, is that there are only two distinctive patterns of life actually possible—two basic outlooks grounded respectively in affirmation of God or in denial of God. Seen aright, philosophy has only two roads. Long years of study and meditation have forced on me the conclusion that this fact dominates our whole human situation, all the jargon of the schools notwithstanding. It is because this fact has been lost sight of in overly voluminous treatises dealing with the human condition, that we are left to deplore with Thomas Hardy "the chronic melancholy which is taking hold of the civilized races." And by this he meant the sense of solitariness which continues to plague our world as it degenerates into a disheartened solitude. Such is the melancholy of a soul which no longer knows how to read the script of its own life.

The clue to the whole problem is disclosed the moment we realize that there is such a thing as a solitary life in the context of the Living God, and a solitary life in the context of ignorance of this God—and by "this God" I mean, the God of Abraham, of Isaac, and of Jacob who supremely revealed Himself in Jesus Christ. All sham and sophistry about solitude must come to naught when this inescapable fact of God in Christ is brought out into the open to strike at the very heart of man's dilatory practices. Having once for all realized the gist of the truth, a man, like the bird struck in mid-flight by an arrow, is "winged" for all time.

Let the solitary man, then, ponder these realities: In a domain beyond the limitations of our infirmity, there is a cosmic drama going on, the meaning of which differs according to whether the God spoken of in the Bible is or is not. Our whole life is at stake in that drama which bears no relation whatsoever to human capacity or initiative—not even to the fact that you and I live to become aware of it. It is just another fact like that of gravitation. And just as we cannot escape our utter dependence on gravitation, so we have no choice but to take sides on the issue at hand. For we are already and utterly involved. Are we *alone* in this universe, or are we not? The clue to the solitary life is to be found right in the answer we give to this question.

The immediate consequence of this, our real condition, is that the aching suspense of a keenly felt solitude proves a delusion in actual life and practice. The way we live and think in the face of a threatening solitude *is* already suggesting the alternative we have already adopted. We *are* in the cast of the cosmic drama. The affirmation or denial of God already animates our own outlook on the solitary life in one way or another. We do not have to emulate Frederic W. H. Myers and put to the Sphinx the question: "Is the universe friendly?" The outlook we have adopted means far more on our part than a profession of faith, or mere lip service to a creed. Our genuine position is not necessarily the one we claim to have; no, not even the one we *think* we have on the deep-seated motivation which causes us to live and move and have our being as we actually do. Suppose you be put on your mettle, cornered in a set of drastic circumstances calling for immediate reaction. How would *you* react? Would that reaction of yours be grounded in the reality of God or in its denial? The question pierces through the very core of our being, possibly through our hypocrisies. Let our first step then be to ask ourselves the question: Does my whole being through feelings, thoughts, actions and reactions—nay, in its most hidden or even unconscious motivation—affirm my utter trust in God or deny it?

A man needs more than mere opinion or even persuasion on this matter. He needs certitude—certitude with reference to the *center* from which all he says, thinks and does proceeds as a river from its spring. But further, he should make sure of what the spring is really like, whether God-centered or self-centered, the self-centeredness of a man being the very essence of what the Bible calls sin—that singular of which there really is no plural.

The Ultimate Spring of Solitude

He who consciously or unconsciously has chosen to ignore God is an orphan in the universe, that is, in God's creation. It is only natural that he should feel lonely to the point of dejection. He may on occasion and for a time seek solace in man-made techniques of self-help. The fact remains, however, that all such techniques take their stand on the purely natural.

They are out of God's context. Their appeal is to some kind of energy and resourcefulness which makes of man the principle and end of all things. Ultimately they are bound to fail and leave a man alone in depression of spirit and heaviness of heart. Thus does self-centeredness generate the bitterness of solitude, as has appeared in a number of our preceding pages. It is just that what God has initiated and what He has given cannot be ignored.

It is such negation of God, and self-centered denial of his own distinctive endowment on the part of man, that the Bible characterizes as sin. Sin's final ground is a pride that repudiates God's purpose. Hence a loss of purposiveness in which we have previously detected a manifestation of solitude. Indeed, self-centeredness defeats its own purpose as freedom *for* God and *in* God is perverted into freedom *from* God.

In this context, then, it does become clear that the ultimate spring of all the miseries born of solitude is sin in the Biblical sense of the word. The soul which has cast its lot with self instead of with God is affected in two essential ways, namely, with reference to will, and with reference to intellect. The will's normal function according to God is to choose, to decide, to act in terms of love. The intellect's normal function is to know what is at stake in terms of right understanding. It stands to reason that when both these functions work according to the wrong approach of self-centeredness, a man no longer loves aright. His position accordingly borders on insanity. He fails to apprehend this created world and he himself as upheld every moment by the sustaining will of God and accordingly dependent on Him for his existence. Details out of context then monopolize his attention as would mere items on a list. The true picture of life is thereby hidden from him. Indeed a man cannot see anything aright apart from the totality to which it belongs as is the case of features in a human face. Hence a sense of alienation and abandonment whose bitter fruit is solitude.

Liberation

We had already come to the conclusion that our first step toward liberation should be to ask ourselves the question: Does my whole being through feelings, thoughts, actions and reactions—nay, in its most hidden or even unconscious motivation—affirm my utter trust in God or deny it? We now have come to the further conclusion that sheer denial, the very essence of sin according to the Bible, is the ultimate spring of all the miseries born of solitude. A man's first need accordingly is liberation from sin—repentance, *metanoia,* a sober, reflective turning of the mind—and salvation, a safe return, *soteria*—the story of the Prodigal Son in action.

What is noteworthy at this point is that the story of the Prodigal Son in itself is also a perfect epic of solitude. We find in it the various phases of experience just pointed out. First, there is the self-centered decision of the boy to live independently from his father. He gathers his share, we are told, then establishes himself in a far country where he lives according to his own code of ethics—if indeed the word "ethics" may be used in his case. Then, as a mighty famine arises in the land where he is left to his own devices, he begins to be in want and soon finds himself in the fields to feed swine. There he goes hungry. His solitude is most dramatically suggested by the statement that "*no man gave unto him.*" Then comes that sober, reflective turning of his mind—repentance, *metanoia:* "I will arise and go to my father, and will say unto him, 'Father, I have sinned against heaven and before thee.' " Whereupon he arises and comes to his *waiting* father. We now witness the safe return, *soteria,* as his father orders that the best robe be brought forth and put on him;

a ring put on his hand, and shoes on his feet; and that the fatted calf be killed so that they might eat and be merry. "For this, my son, was dead, and is alive again; he was lost, and is found."

And so, there is ushered in on the part of the son a life of love and utter dependence upon the father in whose presence he will henceforth live all the days of his life. Gone is the solitude of swine 'feeding! What we now have is an initiation into the practice of the presence of God, the supreme remedy against a relapse into the miseries of solitude.

Specialists do have their day as they advise for solitariness such remedies as continued learning, contributing to our cultural heritage by the practice of trades and arts, joining community groups, helping people in need. To be sure, all such activities are both helpful and praiseworthy. In themselves, however, they carry their stumbling block in that the success of the enterprise depends on the frame of mind in which the lonely approach their task. These pages have led us to characterize solitude as *a state of soul,* and only a soul at peace with God, a soul living every moment in utter dependency upon God can find release from a painful solitude.

George Dawson knew this secret as he devised this prayer (A.D. 1821):

Almighty God, we bless and praise Thee that we have wakened to the light of another earthly day; and now we will think of what a day should be. Our days are Thine, let them be spent for Thee. Our days are few, let them be spent with care. There are dark days behind us, forgive their sinfulness; there may be dark days before us, strengthen us for their trials. We pray Thee to shine on this day, the day which we may call our own. Lord, we go to our daily work, help us to take pleasure therein. Show us clearly what our duty is, help us to be faithful in doing it. Let all we do be well done, fit for Thine eye to see. Give us strength to do, patience to bear, let our courage never fail. When we cannot love our work, let us think of it as Thy task, and by our true love to Thee make unlovely things shine in the light of Thy great love; through Jesus Christ our Lord. Amen.

True prayer, genuine prayer, is a state of being. Let therefore this and similar prayers be *acted* rather than merely uttered. And so it will appear that an authentic solitary life is a life lived *every moment* in love for God and in utter dependence upon Him.

Index of Names